THE BOOK OF FOLLY

THE
BOOK
OF
FOLLY

HOUGHTON MIFFLIN COMPANY BOSTON

ANNE
SEXTON

1973

For Joy,
when she comes to this business of words

✤

Some of the poems in this book have appeared
in *Kayak, Modern Occasions, New American Review, The New Republic, The New York Quarterly,* and *Poetry Australia.*

"The Boat" and "The One-legged Man" originally appeared in *The New Yorker.*

The story "Dancing the Jig" originally appeared in *New American Review.* The story "The Letting Down of the Hair" originally appeared in *The Atlantic Monthly.*

First Printing   c

ISBN: 0–395–14014–5 hardcover; 0–395–14075–7 paperbound; 0–395–14400–0 limited edition
Library of Congress Catalog Card Number: 72–3839
Printed in the United States of America

CONTENTS

I

THIRTY POEMS

THE AMBITION BIRD

So it has come to this —
insomnia at 3:15 A.M.,
the clock tolling its engine

like a frog following
a sundial yet having an electric
seizure at the quarter hour.

The business of words keeps me awake.
I am drinking cocoa,
that warm brown mama.

I would like a simple life
yet all night I am laying
poems away in a long box.

It is my immortality box,
my lay-away plan,
my coffin.

All night dark wings
flopping in my heart.
Each an ambition bird.

The bird wants to be dropped
from a high place like Tallahatchie Bridge.

He wants to light a kitchen match
and immolate himself.

He wants to fly into the hand of Michelangelo
and come out painted on a ceiling.

He wants to pierce the hornet's nest
and come out with a long godhead.

He wants to take bread and wine
and bring forth a man happily floating in the Caribbean.

He wants to be pressed out like a key
so he can unlock the Magi.

He wants to take leave among strangers
passing out bits of his heart like hors d'oeuvres.

He wants to die changing his clothes
and bolt for the sun like a diamond.

He wants, I want.
Dear God, wouldn't it be
good enough to just drink cocoa?

I must get a new bird
and a new immortality box.
There is folly enough inside this one.

THE DOCTOR OF THE HEART

Take away your knowledge, Doktor.
It doesn't butter me up.

You say my heart is *sick unto*.
You ought to have more respect!

You with the goo on the suction cup.
You with your wires and electrodes

fastened at my ankle and wrist,
sucking up the biological breast.

You with your zigzag machine
playing like the stock market up and down.

Give me the Phi Beta key you always twirl
and I will make a gold crown for my molar.

I will take a slug if you please
and make myself a perfectly good appendix.

Give me a fingernail for an eyeglass.
The world was milky all along.

I will take an iron and press out
my slipped disk until it is flat.

But take away my mother's carcinoma
for I have only one cup of fetus tears.

Take away my father's cerebral hemorrhage
for I have only a jigger of blood in my hand.

Take away my sister's broken neck
for I have only my schoolroom ruler for a cure.

Is there such a device for my heart?
I have only a gimmick called magic fingers.

Let me dilate like a bad debt.
Here is a sponge. I can squeeze it myself.

O heart, tobacco red heart,
beat like a rock guitar.

I am at the ship's prow.
I am no longer the suicide

with her raft and paddle.
Herr Doktor! I'll no longer **die**

to spite you, you wallowing
seasick grounded man.

OH

It is snowing and death bugs me
as stubborn as insomnia.
The fierce bubbles of chalk,
the little white lesions
settle on the street outside.
It is snowing and the ninety
year old woman who was combing
out her long white wraith hair
is gone, embalmed even now,
even tonight her arms are smooth
muskets at her side and nothing
issues from her but her last word —
"Oh." Surprised by death.

It is snowing. Paper spots
are falling from the punch.
Hello? Mrs. Death is here!
She suffers according to the digits
of my hate. I hear the filaments
of alabaster. I would lie down
with them and lift my madness
off like a wig. I would lie
outside in a room of wool
and let the snow cover me.
Paris white or flake white
or argentine, all in the washbasin

of my mouth, calling, "Oh."
I am empty. I am witless.
Death is here. There is no
other settlement. Snow!
See the mark, the pock, the pock!

Meanwhile you pour tea
with your handsome gentle hands.
Then you deliberately take your
forefinger and point it at my temple,
saying, "You suicide bitch!
I'd like to take a corkscrew
and screw out all your brains
and you'd never be back ever."
And I close my eyes over the steaming
tea and see God opening His teeth.
"Oh," He says.
I see the child in me writing, "Oh."
Oh, my dear, not why.

SWEENEY

My Sweeney, Mr. Eliot,
is that Australian who came
to the U.S.A. with one thought —
My books in the satchel, my name

and one question at customs —
Is Anne Sexton still alive?
He was a big dollar man, a Monopoly player
who bought up BOARDWALK with a ten or a five

to see the pallid bellboy smile, or please
the maid who supplied nonallergic
pillows. Unlike my father, his mouth a liturgy
of praise. Like a gangster, his wallet a limerick.
Your words, Sexton, are the only

red queens, the only ministers, the only beasts.
You are the altar cup and from this
I do fill my mouth. Sexton, I am your priest.

Sweeney who brought up himself, gone
was his murmurous mother at nine, gone
was his soused-up father at seventeen.
But talkative Sweeney at forty-five lives on.

Lord. Lord. How You leave off. How You eat up men —
leave them walking on the gummy pavements,

sucking in the tamed-up, used-up air,
fearing death and what death invents.

Sweeney from nine to five with a carnation
in his buttonhole introduces the rider
to the cabby; Sweeney who flies through bookshops
not like a turbojet but a Zurich glider.

Ersatz press agent man, buying up my books
by the dozen from Scribner's, Doubleday,
that Italian bookshop or wherever. Fan, fan,
drinking only Dom Perignon, my gray Aussie gourmet.

Yes. Yes. Sweeney gave me all of New York,
caviar at La Côte Basque, a pink shower cap
and death. Yes. That day my sister was killed
and the untimely weapons were unwrapped.

That unnatural death by car, her slim neck
snapped like a piece of celery. A one-week bride,
her dead blue eyes flapping into their solitude
while I drank with Sweeney and her death lied.

Now Sweeney phones from London, W. 2,
saying Martyr, my religion is love, is you.
Be seated, my Sweeney, my invisible fan.
Surely the words will continue, for that's
what's left that's true.

MOTHER AND DAUGHTER

Linda, you are leaving
your old body now.
It lies flat, an old butterfly,
all arm, all leg, all wing,
loose as an old dress.
I reach out toward it but
my fingers turn to cankers
and I am motherwarm and used,
just as your childhood is used.
Question you about this
and you hold up pearls.
Question you about this
and you pass by armies.
Question you about this —
you with your big clock going,
its hands wider than jackstraws —
and you'll sew up a continent.

Now that you are eighteen
I give you my booty, my spoils,
my Mother & Co. and my ailments.
Question you about this
and you'll not know the answer —
the muzzle at the mouth,
the hopeful tent of oxygen,
the tubes, the pathways,

the war and the war's vomit.
Keep on, keep on, keep on,
carrying keepsakes to the boys,
carrying powders to the boys,
carrying, my Linda, blood to
the bloodletter.

Linda, you are leaving
your old body now.
You've picked my pocket clean
and you've racked up all my
poker chips and left me empty
and, as the river between us
narrows, you do calisthenics,
that womanly leggy semaphore.
Question you about this
and you will sew me a shroud
and hold up Monday's broiler
and thumb out the chicken gut.
Question you about this
and you will see my death
drooling at these gray lips
while you, my burglar, will eat
fruit and pass the time of day.

THE WIFEBEATER

There will be mud on the carpet tonight
and blood in the gravy as well.
The wifebeater is out,
the childbeater is out
eating soil and drinking bullets from a cup.
He strides back and forth
in front of my study window
chewing little red pieces of my heart.
His eyes flash like a birthday cake
and he makes bread out of rock.

Yesterday he was walking
like a man in the world.
He was upright and conservative
but somehow evasive, somehow contagious.
Yesterday he built me a country
and laid out a shadow where I could sleep
but today a coffin for the madonna and child,
today two women in baby clothes will be hamburg.

With a tongue like a razor he will kiss,
the mother, the child,
and we three will color the stars black
in memory of his mother
who kept him chained to the food tree
or turned him on and off like a water faucet

and made women through all these hazy years
the enemy with a heart of lies.

Tonight all the red dogs lie down in fear
and the wife and daughter knit into each other
until they are killed.

THE FIREBOMBERS

We are America.
We are the coffin fillers.
We are the grocers of death.
We pack them in crates like cauliflowers.

The bomb opens like a shoebox.
And the child?
The child is certainly not yawning.
And the woman?
The woman is bathing her heart.
It has been torn out of her
and because it is burnt
and as a last act
she is rinsing it off in the river.
This is the death market.

America,
where are your credentials?

THE ONE-LEGGED MAN

Once there was blood
as in a murder
but now there is nothing.

Once there was a shoe,
brown cordovan,
which I tied
and it did me well.

Now
I have given away my leg
to be brought up beside orphans.
I have planted my leg beside the drowned mole
with his fifth pink hand sewn onto his mouth.
I have shipped off my leg so that
it may sink slowly like grit into the Atlantic.
I have jettisoned my leg so that it may
fall out of the sky like immense lumber.
I have eaten my leg so that
it may be spit out like a fingernail.

Yet all along . . .
Yes, all along,
I keep thinking that what I need
to do is buy my leg back.
Surely it is for sale somewhere,

poor broken tool, poor ornament.
It might be in a store somewhere beside a lady's scarf.
I want to write it letters.
I want to feed it supper.
I want to carve a bowstring out of it.
I want to hold it at noon in my bed
and stroke it slowly like a perfect woman.

Lady, lady,
why have you left me?

I did not mean to frighten her.
I wanted only to watch her quietly
as she worked.

THE ASSASSIN

The correct death is written in.
I will fill the need.
My bow is stiff.
My bow is in readiness.
I am the bullet and the hook.
I am cocked and held ready.
In my sights I carve him
like a sculptor. I mold out
his last look at everyone.
I carry his eyes and his
brain bone at every position.
I know his male sex and I do
march over him with my index finger.
His mouth and his anus are one.
I am at the center of feeling.

A subway train is
traveling across my crossbow.
I have a blood bolt
and I have made it mine.
With this man I take in hand
his destiny and with this gun
I take in hand the newspapers and
with my heat I will take him.
He will bend down toward me
and his veins will tumble out

like children . . . Give me
his flag and his eye.
Give me his hard shell and his lip.
He is my evil and my apple and
I will see him home.

GOING GONE

Over stone walls and barns,
miles from the black-eyed Susans,
over circus tents and moon rockets
you are going, going.
You who have inhabited me
in the deepest and most broken place,
are going, going.
An old woman calls up to you
from her deathbed deep in sores,
asking, "What do you keep of her?"
She is the crone in the fables.
She is the fool at the supper
and you, sir, are the traveler.
Although you are in a hurry
you stop to open a small basket
and under layers of petticoats
you show her the tiger-striped eyes
that you have lately plucked,
you show her your specialty, the lips,
those two small bundles,
you show her the two hands
that grip each other fiercely,
one being mine, one being yours.
Torn right off at the wrist bone
when you started in your
impossible going, gone.

Then you place the basket
in the old woman's hollow lap
and as a last act she fondles
these artifacts like a child's head
and murmurs, "Precious. Precious."
And you are glad you have given
them to this one for she too
is making a trip.

ANNA WHO WAS MAD

Anna who was mad,
I have a knife in my armpit.
When I stand on tiptoe I tap out messages.
Am I some sort of infection?
Did I make you go insane?
Did I make the sounds go sour?
Did I tell you to climb out the window?
Forgive. Forgive.
Say not I did.
Say not.
Say.

Speak Mary-words into our pillow.
Take me the gangling twelve-year-old
into your sunken lap.
Whisper like a buttercup.
Eat me. Eat me up like cream pudding.
Take me in.
Take me.
Take.

Give me a report on the condition of my soul.
Give me a complete statement of my actions.
Hand me a jack-in-the-pulpit and let me listen in.
Put me in the stirrups and bring a tour group through.
Number my sins on the grocery list and let me buy.

Did I make you go insane?
Did I turn up your earphone and let a siren drive through?
Did I open the door for the mustached psychiatrist
who dragged you out like a golf cart?
Did I make you go insane?
From the grave write me, Anna!
You are nothing but ashes but nevertheless
pick up the Parker Pen I gave you.
Write me.
Write.

THE HEX

Every time I get happy
the Nana-hex comes through.
Birds turn into plumber's tools,
a sonnet turns into a dirty joke,
a wind turns into a tracheotomy,
a boat turns into a corpse,
a ribbon turns into a noose,
all for the Nana-song,
sour notes calling out in her madness:
You did it. You are the evil.
I was thirteen,
her awkward namesake,
our eyes an identical green.
There is no news in it
except every time I say:
I feel great or
Life is marvelous or
I just wrote a poem,
the heartbeat,
the numb hand,
the eyes going black
from the outer edges,
the xylophone in the ears
and the voice, the voice,
the Nana-hex.
My eyes stutter. I am blind.

Sitting on the stairs at thirteen,
hands fixed over my ears,
the Hitler-mouth psychiatrist climbing
past me like an undertaker,
and the old woman's shriek of fear:
You did it. You are the evil.
It was the day meant for me.
Thirteen for your whole life,
just the masks keep changing.
Blood in my mouth,
a fish flopping in my chest
and doom stamping its little feet.
You did it. You are the evil.
She's long gone.
She went out on the death train.
But someone is in the shooting gallery
biding her time.
The dead take aim.
I feel great!
Life is marvelous!
and yet bull's eye,
the hex.

It's all a matter of history.
Brandy is no solace.
Librium only lies me down
like a dead snow queen.
Yes! I am still the criminal.
Yes! Take me to the station house.
But book my double.

DREAMING THE BREASTS

Mother,
strange goddess face
above my milk home,
that delicate asylum,
I ate you up.
All my need took
you down like a meal.

What you gave
I remember in a dream:
the freckled arms binding me,
the laugh somewhere over my woolly hat,
the blood fingers tying my shoe,
the breasts hanging like two bats
and then darting at me,
bending me down.

The breasts I knew at midnight
beat like the sea in me now.
Mother, I put bees in my mouth
to keep from eating
yet it did you no good.
In the end they cut off your breasts
and milk poured from them
into the surgeon's hand
and he embraced them.

I took them from him
and planted them.

I have put a padlock
on you, Mother, dear dead human,
so that your great bells,
those dear white ponies,
can go galloping, galloping,
wherever you are.

THE RED SHOES

I stand in the ring
in the dead city
and tie on the red shoes.
Everything that was calm
is mine, the watch with an ant walking,
the toes, lined up like dogs,
the stove long before it boils toads,
the parlor, white in winter, long before flies,
the doe lying down on moss, long before the bullet.
I tie on the red shoes.

They are not mine.
They are my mother's.
Her mother's before.
Handed down like an heirloom
but hidden like shameful letters.
The house and the street where they belong
are hidden and all the women, too,
are hidden.

All those girls
who wore the red shoes,
each boarded a train that would not stop.
Stations flew by like suitors and would not stop.
They all danced like trout on the hook.
They were played with.

They tore off their ears like safety pins.
Their arms fell off them and became hats.
Their heads rolled off and sang down the street.
And their feet — oh God, their feet in the market place —
their feet, those two beetles, ran for the corner
and then danced forth as if they were proud.
Surely, people exclaimed,
surely they are mechanical. Otherwise . . .

But the feet went on.
The feet could not stop.
They were wound up like a cobra that sees you.
They were elastic pulling itself in two.
They were islands during an earthquake.
They were ships colliding and going down.
Never mind you and me.
They could not listen.
They could not stop.
What they did was the death dance.

What they did would do them in.

THE OTHER

Under my bowels, yellow with smoke,
it waits.
Under my eyes, those milk bunnies,
it waits.
It is waiting.
It is waiting.
Mr. Doppelgänger. My brother. My spouse.
Mr. Doppelgänger. My enemy. My lover.
When truth comes spilling out like peas
it hangs up the phone.
When the child is soothed and resting on the breast
it is my other who swallows Lysol.
When someone kisses someone or flushes the toilet
it is my other who sits in a ball and cries.
My other beats a tin drum in my heart.
My other hangs up laundry as I try to sleep.
My other cries and cries and cries
when I put on a cocktail dress.
It cries when I prick a potato.
It cries when I kiss someone hello.
It cries and cries and cries
until I put on a painted mask
and leer at Jesus in His passion.
Then it giggles.
It is a thumbscrew.
Its hatred makes it clairvoyant.

I can only sign over everything,
the house, the dog, the ladders, the jewels,
the soul, the family tree, the mailbox.

Then I can sleep.

Maybe.

THE SILENCE

*"The more I write, the more the silence seems
to be eating away at me."* C. K. Williams

My room is whitewashed,
as white as a rural station house
and just as silent;
whiter than chicken bones
bleaching in the moonlight,
pure garbage,
and just as silent.
There is a white statue behind me
and white plants
growing like obscene virgins,
pushing out their rubbery tongues
but saying nothing.

My hair is the one dark.
It has been burnt in the white fire
and is just a char.
My beads too are black,
twenty eyes heaved up
from the volcano,
quite contorted.

I am filling the room
with the words from my pen.
Words leak out of it like a miscarriage.
I am zinging words out into the air
and they come back like squash balls.

Yet there is silence.
Always silence.
Like an enormous baby mouth.

The silence is death.
It comes each day with its shock
to sit on my shoulder, a white bird,
and peck at the black eyes
and the vibrating red muscle
of my mouth.

THE HOARDER

"An idler is like a lump of dung; whoever picks
it up shakes it off his hand." Ecclesiasticus

There is something there
I've got to get and I dig
down and people pop off and
muskrats float up backward
and open at my touch like
cereal flakes and still I've
got to dig because there is
something down there in my
Nana's clock I broke it I was
wrong I was digging even then
I had to find out and snap
and crack the hand broke like
a toothpick and I didn't learn
I keep digging for something
down there is my sister's five
dollar bill that I tore because
it wasn't mine was stage money
wasn't mine something down there
I am digging I am digging I will
win something like my first bike
teetering my first balancing act
a grasshopper who can fly she
of the damp smelling passageway
it was earlier much earlier it
was my first doll that water went
into and water came out of much

earlier it was the diaper I wore
and the dirt thereof and my
mother hating me for it and me
loving me for it but the hate
won didn't it yes the distaste
won the disgust won and because
of this I am a hoarder of words
I hold them in though they are
dung oh God I am a digger
I am not an idler
am I?

KILLING THE SPRING

"When the cold rains kept on and killed the
spring, it was as though a young person had died
for no reason." Ernest Hemingway, A Moveable Feast

Spring had been bulldozed under.
She would not, would not, would not.
Late April, late May
and the metallic rains kept on.
From my gun-metal window I watched
how the dreadful tulips
swung on their hinges,
beaten down like pigeons.

Then I ignored spring.
I put on blinders and rode on a donkey
in a circle, a warm circle.
I tried to ride for eternity
but I came back.
I swallowed my sour meat
but it came back.
I struck out memory with an X
but it came back.
I tied down time with a rope
but it came back.

Then
I put my head in a death bowl
and my eyes shut up like clams.
They didn't come back.

I was declared legally blind
by my books and papers.
My eyes, those two blue gods,
would not come back.
My eyes, those sluts, those whores,
would play no more.

Next I nailed my hands
onto a pine box.
I followed the blue veins
like a neon road map.
My hands, those touchers, those bears,
would not reach out and speak.
They could no longer get in the act.
They were fastened down to oblivion.
They did not come back.
They were through with their abominable habits.
They were in training for a crucifixion.
They could not reply.

Next I took my ears,
those two cold moons,
and drowned them in the Atlantic.
They were not wearing a mask.
They were not deceived by laughter.
They were not luminous like the clock.
They sank like oiled birds.
They did not come back.
I waited with my bones on the cliff
to see if they'd float in like slick
but they did not come back.

I could not see the spring.
I could not hear the spring.

I could not touch the spring.
Once upon a time a young person
died for no reason.
I was the same.

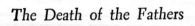

The Death *of the* Fathers

1. OYSTERS

Oysters we ate,
sweet blue babies,
twelve eyes looked up at me,
running with lemon and Tabasco.
I was afraid to eat this father-food
and Father laughed
and drank down his martini,
clear as tears.
It was a soft medicine
that came from the sea into my mouth,
moist and plump.
I swallowed.
It went down like a large pudding.
Then I ate one o'clock and two o'clock.
Then I laughed and then we laughed
and let me take note —
there was a death,
the death of childhood
there at the Union Oyster House
for I was fifteen
and eating oysters
and the child was defeated.
The woman won.

2. HOW WE DANCED

The night of my cousin's wedding
I wore blue.
I was nineteen
and we danced, Father, we orbited.
We moved like angels washing themselves.
We moved like two birds on fire.
Then we moved like the sea in a jar,
slower and slower.
The orchestra played
"Oh how we danced on the night we were wed."
And you waltzed me like a lazy Susan
and we were dear,
very dear.
Now that you are laid out,
useless as a blind dog,
now that you no longer lurk,
the song rings in my head.
Pure oxygen was the champagne we drank
and clicked our glasses, one to one.
The champagne breathed like a skin diver
and the glasses were crystal and the bride
and groom gripped each other in sleep
like nineteen-thirty marathon dancers.
Mother was a belle and danced with twenty men.
You danced with me never saying a word.
Instead the serpent spoke as you held me close.

The serpent, that mocker, woke up and pressed against me
like a great god and we bent together
like two lonely swans.

3. THE BOAT

Father
(he calls himself
"old sea dog"),
in his yachting cap
at the wheel of the Chris-Craft,
a mahogany speedboat
named Go Too III,
speeds out past Cuckold's Light
over the dark brainy blue.
I in the very back
with an orange life jacket on.
I in the dare seat.
Mother up front.
Her kerchief flapping.
The waves deep as whales.
(Whales in fact have been sighted.
A school two miles out of Boothbay Harbor.)
It is bumpy and we are going too fast.
The waves are boulders that we ride upon.
I am seven and we are riding
to Pemaquid or Spain.
Now the waves are higher;
they are round buildings.
We start to go through them
and the boat shudders.
Father is going faster.

I am wet.
I am tumbling on my seat
like a loose kumquat.
Suddenly
a wave that we go under.
Under. Under. Under.
We are daring the sea.
We have parted it.
We are scissors.
Here in the green room
the dead are very close.
Here in the pitiless green
where there are no keepsakes
or cathedrals an angel spoke:
You have no business.
No business here.
Give me a sign,
cries Father,
and the sky breaks over us.
There is air to have.
There are gulls kissing the boat.
There is the sun as big as a nose.
And here are the three of us
dividing our deaths,
bailing the boat
and closing out
the cold wing that has clasped us
this bright August day.

4. SANTA

Father,
the Santa Claus suit
you bought from Wolff Fording Theatrical Supplies,
back before I was born,
is dead.
The white beard you fooled me with
and the hair like Moses,
the thick crimpy wool
that used to buzz me on the neck,
is dead.
Yes, my busting rosy Santa,
ringing your bronze cowbell.
You with real soot on your nose
and snow (taken from the refrigerator some years)
on your big shoulder.
The room was like Florida.
You took so many oranges out of your bag
and threw them around the living room,
all the time laughing that North Pole laugh.
Mother would kiss you
for she was that tall.
Mother could hug you
for she was not afraid.
The reindeer pounded on the roof.
(It was my Nana with a hammer in the attic.
For my children it was my husband

with a crowbar breaking things up.)
The year I ceased to believe in you
is the year you were drunk.
My boozy red man,
your voice all slithery like soap,
you were a long way from Saint Nick
with Daddy's cocktail smell.
I cried and ran from the room
and you said, "Well, thank God that's over!"
And it was, until the grandchildren came.
Then I tied up your pillows
in the five A.M. Christ morning
and I adjusted the beard,
all yellow with age,
and applied rouge to your cheeks
and Chalk White to your eyebrows.
We were conspirators,
secret actors,
and I kissed you
because I was tall enough.
But that is over.
The era closes
and large children hang their stockings
and build a black memorial to you.
And you, you fade out of sight
like a lost signalman
wagging his lantern
for the train that comes no more.

5. FRIENDS

Father,
who were all those friends,
that one in particular,
an oily creature,
who kept my picture in his wallet
and would show it to me
in secret like something dirty?
He used to sing to me,
I saw a little fly
and he buzzed me on the cheek.
I'd like to see that little fly
kiss our Annie every week.
And then he'd buzz,
on the cheek,
on the buttocks.
Or else he'd take a car
and run it up my back.
Or else he'd blow some whiskey
in my mouth, all dark and suede.
Who was he, Father?
What right, Father?
To pick me up like Charlie McCarthy
and place me on his lap?
He was as bald as a hump.
His ears stuck out like teacups
and his tongue, my God, his tongue,

like a red worm and when he kissed
it crawled right in.

Oh Father, Father,
who was that stranger
who knew Mother too well?
And he made me jump rope
five hundred times,
calling out,
Little one, jump higher, higher,
dragging me up and pushing me down
when it was you, Father,
who had the right
and ought.
He was beating me on the buttocks
with a jump rope.
I was stained with his red fingers
and I cried out for you
and Mother said you were gone on a trip.
You had sunk like the cat in the snow,
not a paw left to clasp for luck.
My heart cracked like a doll-dish,
my heart seized like a bee sting,
my eyes filled up like an owl,
and my legs crossed themselves like Christ's.
He was a stranger, Father.
Oh God,
he was a stranger,
was he not?

6. BEGAT

Father me not
for you are not my father.
Today there is that doubt.
Today there is that monster between us,
that monster of doubt.
Today someone else lurks in the wings
with your dear lines in his mouth
and your crown on his head.
Oh Father, Father-sorrow,
where has time brought us?

Today someone called.
"Merry Christmas," said the stranger.
"I am your real father."
That was a knife.
That was a grave.
That was a ship sailing through my heart.
From the galley I heard the slaves
calling out, *Fall* away, *fall* away.
And again I heard the stranger's
"I am your real father."

Was I transplanted?
Father, Father,
where is your tendril?
Where was the soil?

Who was the bee?
Where was the moment?

A courtesy uncle called —
that stranger —
and claimed me in my forty-second year.
Now I am a true blue,
as sure as a buffalo
and as mad as a salmon.
Illegitimate at last.
Father,
adored every night but one,
cuckolded that once,
the night of my conception
in that flapper way,
tell me, old dead thing,
where were you when Mother
swallowed me down whole?
Where were you, old fox,
two brown eyes, two moles,
hiding under your liquor
soft as oil?

Where was I begat?
In what room did
those definitive juices come?
A hotel in Boston
gilt and dim?
Was it a February night
all wrapped in fur
that knew me not?
I ask this.
I sicken.

Father,
you died once,
salted down at fifty-nine,
packed down like a big snow angel,
wasn't that enough?
To appear again and die out of me.
To take away your manic talking,
your broomstick legs, all those
familial resemblances we shared.
To take the you out of the me.
To send me into the genes
of this explorer.
He will hold me at knife point
and like a knife blade I will say:
Stranger,
bone to my bone man,
go your way.
I say take your sperm,
it is old,
it has turned to acid,
it will do you no good.

Stranger,
stranger,
take away your riddle.
Give it to a medical school
for I sicken.
My loss knocks.

For here stands my father,
a rosy Santa,
telling the old Rumpelstiltskin to me,
larger than God or the Devil.

He is my history.
I see him standing on the snowbank
on Christmas Eve
singing "Good King Wenceslas"
to the white, glowering houses
or giving Mother rubies to put in her eyes,
red, red, Mother, you are blood red.
He scoops her up in his arms
all red shivers and silks.
He cries to her:
How dare I hold this princess?
A mere man such as I
with a shark's nose and ten tar-fingers?
Princess of the artichokes,
my dickeybird,
my dolly mop,
my kiddley wink,
my jill of the jacks,
my rabbit pie!
And they kissed until I turned away.
Sometimes even I came into the royal ring
and those times he ate my heart in half
and I was glad.
Those times I smelled the Vitalis on his pajamas.
Those times I mussed his curly black hair
and touched his ten tar-fingers
and swallowed down his whiskey breath.
Red. Red. Father, you are blood red.
Father,
we are two birds on fire.

Angels of the Love Affair

"Angels of the love affair, do you know
that other, the dark one, that other me?"

1. ANGEL OF FIRE AND GENITALS

Angel of fire and genitals, do you know slime,
that green mama who first forced me to sing,
who put me first in the latrine, that pantomime
of brown where I was beggar and she was king?
I said, "The devil is down that festering hole."
Then he bit me in the buttocks and took over my soul.

Fire woman, you of the ancient flame, you
of the Bunsen burner, you of the candle,
you of the blast furnace, you of the barbecue,
you of the fierce solar energy, Mademoiselle,
take some ice, take some snow, take a month of rain
and you would gutter in the dark, cracking up your brain.

Mother of fire, let me stand at your devouring gate
as the sun dies in your arms and you loosen its terrible
     weight.

2. ANGEL OF CLEAN SHEETS

Angel of clean sheets, do you know bedbugs?
Once in a madhouse they came like specks of cinnamon
as I lay in a chloral cave of drugs,
as old as a dog, as quiet as a skeleton.
Little bits of dried blood. One hundred marks
upon the sheet. One hundred kisses in the dark.

White sheets smelling of soap and Clorox
have nothing to do with this night of soil,
nothing to do with barred windows and multiple locks
and all the webbing in the bed, the ultimate recoil.
I have slept in silk and in red and in black.
I have slept on sand and, one fall night, a haystack.

I have known a crib. I have known the tuck-in of a child
but inside my hair waits the night I was defiled.

3. ANGEL OF FLIGHT AND SLEIGH BELLS

Angel of flight and sleigh bells, do you know paralysis,
that ether house where your arms and legs are cement?
You are as still as a yardstick. You have a doll's kiss.
The brain whirls in a fit. The brain is not evident.
I have gone to that same place without a germ or a stroke.
A little solo act — that lady with the brain that broke.

In this fashion I have become a tree.
I have become a vase you can pick up or drop at will,
inanimate at last. What unusual luck! My body
passively resisting. Part of the leftovers. Part of the kill.
Angel of flight, you soarer, you flapper, you floater,
you gull that grows out of my back in the dreams I prefer,

stay near. But give me the totem. Give me the shut eye
where I stand in stone shoes as the world's bicycle goes by.

4. ANGEL OF HOPE AND CALENDARS

Angel of hope and calendars, do you know despair?
That hole I crawl into with a box of Kleenex,
that hole where the fire woman is tied to her chair,
that hole where leather men are wringing their necks,
where the sea has turned into a pond of urine.
There is no place to wash and no marine beings to stir in.

In this hole your mother is crying out each day.
Your father is eating cake and digging her grave.
In this hole your baby is strangling. Your mouth is clay.
Your eyes are made of glass. They break. You are not brave.
You are alone like a dog in a kennel. Your hands
break out in boils. Your arms are cut and bound by bands

of wire. Your voice is out there. Your voice is strange.
There are no prayers here. Here there is no change.

5. ANGEL OF BLIZZARDS AND BLACKOUTS

Angel of blizzards and blackouts, do you know raspberries,
those rubies that sat in the green of my grandfather's
    garden?
You of the snow tires, you of the sugary wings, you freeze
me out. Let me crawl through the patch. Let me be ten.
Let me pick those sweet kisses, thief that I was,
as the sea on my left slapped its applause.

Only my grandfather was allowed there. Or the maid
who came with a scullery pan to pick for breakfast.
She of the rolls that floated in the air, she of the inlaid
woodwork all greasy with lemon, she of the feather and
    dust,
not I. Nonetheless I came sneaking across the salt lawn
in bare feet and jumping-jack pajamas in the spongy dawn.

Oh Angel of the blizzard and blackout, Madam white face,
take me back to that red mouth, that July 21st place.

6. ANGEL OF BEACH HOUSES AND PICNICS

Angel of beach houses and picnics, do you know solitaire?
Fifty-two reds and blacks and only myself to blame.
My blood buzzes like a hornet's nest. I sit in a kitchen chair
at a table set for one. The silverware is the same
and the glass and the sugar bowl. I hear my lungs fill and
     expel
as in an operation. But I have no one left to tell.

Once I was a couple. I was my own king and queen
with cheese and bread and rosé on the rocks of Rockport.
Once I sunbathed in the buff, all brown and lean,
watching the toy sloops go by, holding court
for busloads of tourists. Once I called breakfast the sexiest
meal of the day. Once I invited arrest

at the peace march in Washington. Once I was young and
     bold
and left hundreds of unmatched people out in the cold.

II

THREE STORIES

DANCING THE JIG

What I want to talk about is dancing the jig. It is very strange to dance the jig. I am doing it now. My hands jolt from my wrists, my elbows fly from my shoulders, my head twists from my waist and my legs leap over the people on the floor. Oh, I am dancing, dancing. Before this I was sitting on the floor with the others. I am at a party. When they put the music on I began to feel lively, very lively. My nerves began to tick like a French clock, chimes rang from my fingers, my feet began to tap tap upon the floor and my toes curled in my shoes. I was up on my knees with my hands swinging out in frantic circles over my head and my head itself rolled on its hinges. Oh, I didn't like it. I didn't want to . . . But here I am, cavorting over their silent faces. They are blobs of jelly. I think I have eaten the music. It runs through me as if I had swallowed it whole. The music, the music — bounce! I am the music fisting around. We are the beat and balance of the air. My dress flutters around me. I think I had better stop, but I cannot. My legs seem numb but they still hurry me into their frolic. The sound pulls me like a puppet on sixteen different strings. They are very clever, these sounds of the voices of the music. Oh, the little moving staircase of sound — I hate it. But, see! I am dancing the jig.

Now the music has gone. I pitch back to the floor. Everyone pretends not to notice. Sweat pours down me. I shut my eyes, trying not to think of how I have just acted. I am ashamed. I am wondering why I have to. I know that this has happened before in other places and other years. What can be wrong with me? Why do I suddenly and always leap out and start that dance? Someone is passing me a glass on the left. I take it in my hand. I am drinking now and trying to think . . .

You know how it is at a party, that moment in the conversation when someone gets up to fix another drink. The room is silent and smoky. No one speaks and you let your eyes stare off and see double. You allow your eyes to go; you want your eyes to go; you prefer, for instance, to observe a chair. Look at it! Its color, the streak of the grain, the soft shadows, the stiff arms in their places, the four legs hitting the floor. Nothing is more important than the chair. You can see it and see it twice. Then someone moves, speaks, fills your glass and the room squares back as the mouths move and the eyes focus. Have your eyes really come back or have you lost them to the chair? I think I give mine away. This must be the danger point — the chair. I think it begins here, but I'm not sure. Is this some sickness? Am I so odd? I am sure that everyone does some sort of staring trick. But they come back. Perhaps I let myself become overconfident; perhaps I shouldn't try to become the chair. Other people probably do it differently. But they are not afraid. Why did I say afraid? I am not afraid.

I'm bored: bored with the party, with the people, with myself. Or maybe I used the word afraid because I am. I'm scared. Not of the chair; of the total, of the party that makes my eyes a chair . . . a chair that is so mindless that finally I must eat music. I am distant, as plain as a chair, as unmoved, as unnoticeable. The chair says, Don't look at me, I am nothing. The chair says, I stay the same, sit on me, crack my legs, lean on my arms, but I will not move. Yes, that's just what I like about a chair, about being a chair. But it doesn't work. The opposite of chair is dancing the jig.

Tonight when I became the chair, I thought, No one notices

it. No one will see. I reply to someone. I smile. I am drinking and looking off. I put my left hand into my pocketbook and fish for a cigarette. I do not need to watch my hands. They know their way past a wallet, pencils, three lipsticks, a loose cigarette. I pull up, noting that my hand is heavy and numb. I place the soft white stick in my mouth. I ask if he has a light. He does. The match strikes and I lean toward its redness. I am still seeing double. I am very distant, but no one can see this. I am fooling them still. Maybe they think I am drunk. Probably they are drunk. Everyone speaks slowly and faraway. I can count four different conversations from the couples who are sitting on the floor near me. I know without looking just what they look like and that they do not notice me. I have another drink now. I taste the drink. Can a chair taste?

That's my worst mistake, thinking I am a chair, trying to stay fixed. I try so that I won't move, won't take the music, won't dance the jig. I try to stay fixed. But I never do. Sometimes I have tried pictures on the wall, or candlelight, seeing the flame double. I remember, when I was little, that I used to stare at my napkin ring at the dinner table. Maybe the party reminds me of the dinner table? There was always a loud conversation going on. Why do I come from such a talkative family? I hated mealtimes: the white cloth, the silver serving dishes reflecting the candles and our faces, the glasses filled with floating ice, the smoke from Mother's ashtray, the maid on the left passing squash and potatoes. I had a round napkin ring with my name on it. It was silver. I used to stare at it.

Silver shines right into your eyes and your eyes are a mirror that shines back into it. She would talk to me with food in her mouth and I could hear her thick breath going up and down through her nostrils. I try not to hear her. I can taste the sound of her voice. She is angry. Her words slip out between bits;

they run out as if her food were spilling back out between her lips. I don't listen. I look down at my napkin ring. I hold it like a mirror and an object of escape, an object to see twice. Fascinated. I shine. I don't care. It doesn't matter, but I wish she would stop. I am somewhere else. The others are talking. Mother will cut my meat. She is talking and cutting it. I hate meat. My sisters groan and giggle. *Mother, Mother, don't cut her meat. She is old enough.* I hear them a little. I am old enough. I am older than I was. I think I am ten or twelve. I don't wear lipstick and I don't have any breasts. But I am tall. I am as tall as Mother. I don't say anything and Mother is cutting my meat. She is still chewing. I am spinning my napkin ring between my fingers. It is very smooth. We shine. I am a napkin ring. I go around and around. I see two napkin rings going around and around. Oh! She snaps my fingers with her nails. It stings. She takes the napkin ring and puts it beside her place and then puts my plate back in front of me. Soon she will be done eating and then she will smoke. The napkin ring is gone and I must eat my meat. I try not to listen to her. If I listen to her I will become her. It is hard to think. The napkin ring is gone. I chew. I try to think. Oh. No. I try not to think. I mustn't think that my mouth is her mouth and that I am breathing through her nostrils. My sisters are talking. My father, at the end of the table, is drunk. I do not know that he is drunk. I think he is cross. I always think things are different from what they really are. I am too young to know that he is drunk. I will know it someday.

Mother is still talking. I am eating meat. I try not to look at the meat. I am trying to — She thinks my hair is terrible. I touch it. It doesn't feel terrible. It feels nice, like silk. I twirl a string of it. She says it is too long. She is chewing and I am chewing and I am chewing and twirling my hair. I wish I could sit somewhere else. Part of me is running and the other part is sitting here frozen to the chair. I am still chewing. I am the youngest but I am not little. She is talking about my hair. My father thinks it is a mess too. My sisters don't look at me. They look at each other. My father is cross. He talks from faraway. I can see his face between the candles and it is very fat and red. He doesn't eat much. His eyes are slits that gleam down, two angry black beads. I don't look at Mother's eyes. She snaps my fingers with her nails. I must stop fooling with my hair! I am trying to eat my meat. It takes so much chewing. I think it is stuck in my throat. I look at Mother; I try not to look at her nostrils. She is talking about my sweater because it is dirty. My sisters each make a face at me. I am very thin. Even a clean sweater wouldn't help. I don't know this now, but it is true. I am beginning to watch Mother and watch her words coming out. I am trying to answer but I must be very careful with this meat in my mouth. Now I am talking. I am trying to change the subject; trying to keep control. I look at her hands. They are covered with rings that sparkle and move. I don't want to cry. I am trying to swallow. She is talking again. The maid is taking out the plates. She doesn't take mine because I haven't finished my dinner. I am working on it, bite by bite. I wish Mother would smile. She is lighting a cigarette. Maybe it will be easier now that she is done eating. Maybe if I could think of something else — something nice — then I would feel better. Nana! I am thinking of Nana. Nana is nice.

But Nana is upstairs. She is in her room. She doesn't feel well anymore. She is crazy but I don't know it. I just know that she is different. She moans and paces up and down her room. She has her own living room up there. I like it in her room. She has a blue couch and a copper teapot on the table. It is a squashy couch and I take naps with Nana or play rummy with Nana. Nana eats very nicely. But now she is sick. She doesn't come down to the table. When I do go up to her room, where we used to tell secrets and be comfy, she won't sit down with me. I will sit on her couch and try to talk with her, but she will only moan, pacing back and forth from wall to wall, twisting her veiny old hands and mumbling to herself. She won't smile. She used to. I don't understand about people being different when they were your friend yesterday.

I am thinking about Nana who is kind, but different now, and I am chewing and chewing. The maid is serving dessert. The maid is very quiet, as if she were wearing sneakers. Her lips are thin and pressed tight. Mother is talking. I am starting to talk myself. The words are running out of my mouth and she is catching them and hurling them back at me. My eyes are beginning to smart, the candlelight hurts. It is starting now — I can feel it begin and I can't help myself. I am trying to chew and the meat and the words get mixed up together. Her nostrils. She is eating pudding. It works soft and muddy between her lips. I am talking again. I shouldn't be; I shouldn't have thought of Nana who is upstairs or of Daddy who is cross or of my ugly hair or my ugly sweater or of talking and now I am saying things and I am talking right into the meat. I feel my arms begin to twitch, relentlessly pushing back and forth, plate to mouth, plate to mouth. Chew. Chew. Chew. Mother is talking. I am talking. My arms move like a shuttle. My lips move on words and meat. I can't control anything. My words are her words. My mouth is her mouth. I can only watch myself and feel ashamed. I am not going to cry. It is better to talk than to cry. She thinks I am going to cry. There is food in my throat and my arm is holding my hand that grips the fork that moves. We are going back and forth, chewing, eating. Mother! Mother is smoking. I try to get up and run away but I cannot move away. I can hear my nostrils. I can hear my mouth. I can hear everyone laughing at me. Mother is smiling now but she is blurred. I am afraid I am crying. I feel it start in my throat and the smell of my tears, meaty tears, disgusts me. I can't swallow. My hands are eating and tears are running down my face and out of my nostrils. *All right, Mother, you win!* . . . I gag it out. I am still trying to chew although I am crying. *Win? Win what?* I hear her through her cigarette smoke. She is turning away now. I feel the awful tears but she isn't looking anymore. I guess she is done for tonight.

Now my plate is gone. She is talking to my father who is red and to my sisters who are moving their faces. They are talking about Nana, about sending Nana away. I do not understand what they mean. I do not understand why people change. I do not even understand that I have just danced the jig. It is over now. My dessert is served on the left by the maid.

My eyes blink at the lights of the party. I have been thinking while my glass grew hollow and warm in my hands. It is better not to think. I do not understand why people continue to change; why even I, who am afraid to change at all, change most. Oh, I could blame them all then, if I were little. Now, it is different. Can I blame the music, the chair, the faces at the party? Why do I leap up and start that dance? I can't think of it! I'll look at that chair, at its color, the streak of its grain, the smooth shadows, the stiff arms in their places, the four legs hitting the floor. I can see it. I can see it double! It is fine. No one notices this. No one sees how it is. It is a relief to dwell on it — a perfect object. So fixed. So always the same.

THE BALLET OF THE BUFFOON

The Buffoon and His Wife

In the beginning there was only the buffoon. There was his
wife, of course. But she was another matter. She kept chang-
ing back and forth. She kept pretending to die and then being
resurrected. She was a strange one. One might say she had a
calling. Death and then rebirth. A calling indeed.

The buffoon was a clever fellow. He was a liar. He was also
a poet. He was always planting a broomstick and promising
leaves. He had many devices. He was always using a frozen
carp for an ax. And such and such. And it worked, of course.
A clever fellow. Some thought him a fool. Some thought him
a bishop. He answered to both. Once he held three stones in
his mouth and said, "I am the Trinity." And they believed.
Sometimes when he met a townsman he would climb up him
and call it a ballet. And it was. A ballet of sorts. The towns-
people called him Mr. Ha-ha.

He had, he told them, a miraculous whip that could raise
the dead. Seven townsmen gathered around to see. His wife
was on the floor as dead as a flatiron. Or so he said. "Poor
wife," he went on. "What a gloom. But with my whip I can
resurrect her. My whip is a traveler who brings forth life." He
whipped. He whipped. It lashed around her like a snake. The
day was dark and long. Again he lashed out at her and she rose
up all milk and yellowy hair and kissed him on the cheek.
What a scene! What a shriek! What a Nazi death camp in
reverse!

"Ah ha," cried the townsmen, "we will buy that whip."

And buy it they did. "Now we will have the pleasure of killing our wives. They've irritated. They've bossed. They've collected bills. They've neglected. They've teased and put coal in our coffee. But now we can kill them! We thank you, dear Mr. Ha-ha."

Thus they too became buffoons.

Dance of the Buffoons' Wives

The wives gathered like a bunch of orphans. They were afraid. They knew the whip was not miraculous. "We will not rise from the dead like Lazarus, that much we know." And so each one did a dance. A death dance. A dance before God.

The first wife said, "I am running like a greyhound. I am a hard wind. And I am panting and snapping so that I will not go down."

The second wife said, "I am held. I can only slap in two. I am a book that keeps slamming shut. Then someone opens me and I slam again like a poltergeist."

The third wife said, "I cannot die. I am the wanton. I am swinging my nightgown back and forth. I am all film and tongue and flower. He would not dare!"

The fourth wife said, "I am adrift like a large floating hand. He will not see me go by. I am a pale wing that slips by unnoticed."

The fifth wife said, "I am a snowball waiting for the end. I am all wrapped up like a two-year-old. I am in a huddle and I am snugged into my tiny bones."

The sixth wife said, "I'm on my toes, quickly, quickly. I am walking on fire. It sizzles beneath me like bees. I am walking on fire like a trapeze artist. My foot is already dead."

The seventh wife said, "I am a fly in the snow whirring again and again against the warm windowpane. My parts are wearing out. I have outlived my time."

They stopped their dance and spoke in unison. "Come, husbands. We are ready. We are soft so melt us down."

The Buffoons Kill Their Wives

It was like one long dream. The seven buffoons became seven assassins. They came to their wives licking their guns. They came forth for their prizes, each singing a suffering lullaby. They were swollen with their wanting. They were swollen and alive with their killing. No one spoke a word. The silence was God's silence. Their targets were already lonely for their deaths. Like the course of a disease they had danced through their deaths. The bullets came. The wives were not covered. They did not cringe. The bullets dazzled their heads like a crown of thorns and then they simply lay down like limp laundry. From their husbands they were awfully parted.

The husbands were enjoying their freedom. They hung around and had a kind of bachelor dinner. Claret, a rack of lamb and cockleberry pie. Dusk fell.

"Can it be that simple?" asked one of the buffoons.

The rest laughed. It was a dark laughter.

Then another said, "It is night. It is the time of the wife." And he spoke to her body. "Come, my buttercup. I will whip you awake."

Then all the whips sang like babies. Each man resurrecting his wife. The husbands married that beating, that berserk resurrection.

But the wives lay as still as flatirons. They did not get up again and put on their smiles. Their voices were folded under their arms and even their pain would not crawl out. Even their fingerprints went home. They had been alive without knowing why. They had been young and old without knowing why. They had been jammed into their bodies without knowing why. Now they were stone angels with neither a dime nor a kiss-off.

That was the end of that. The buffoons were widowers. All the woman in them was gone. There was no theory. There was only death.

And Mr. Ha-ha ran from them calling out, "That was your finest hour. Your lyric moment. Now don't complain."

Since they could not catch him, they gutted their hearts and went on somehow.

The Buffoon Dressed as a Young Wife

I will never be caught, thought Mr. Ha-ha as he dressed himself in his sister's clothes. A little rouge, a little frill at the neck. A red wig, a dozy red wig. Quite comely in fact. Now I am my sister, he proclaimed to the mirror.

He then came forth and proclaimed he was Mr. Ha-ha's sister and the buffoons believed him. One of the buffoons hired him as his cook since he no longer had a wife to do for him.

I am as anonymous as the cabbage I cook for supper, thought Mr. Ha-ha. I am the most miraculous man of all. I am the biggest man. I am Big Ben. I am the smallest woman. I am a Dixie cup. I'm the heart's whole satisfaction. I'm a throb of a woman. And he was.

Third Entr'acte

From the beginning it was Mr. Ha-ha's song. He had the personality for it.

He sang: "They thought I was a dummy, a greenhorn, a chap who can't come up with the big figure, but I'm on to them and their fat-witted ways. I'm a king. I'm a queen. I'm Mr. Bone Bag. I'm a dish of gooseberries, and they are invalids. My feet are slier than their tongues. My arms are darling but my hands are butchers. I live by my wits for I'm a betting man. I'm as strong as red meat. I'm the knave of trumps. I pump thunder and make a hell broth."

As you can see, the merchant was smitten. His mother, some say, was deaf and never answered his letters. His sister was an overpowering thing, younger of course, always knocking down his blocks. A little dictator. The merchant had, at last, his own wench. To do with, he thought, as he would.

Mr. Ha-ha was anxious. Transvestite that he was. A curious eye was approaching. The penultimate hour was upon him.

"A hand of cards," Mr. Ha-ha suggested. "A little croquet on the lawn? Cat's cradle so that our fingers may get acquainted."

"None of these, my wife. You will not escape. You will not go fast asleep over your games tonight, my wife. Nor will you crawl into your cubbyhole. We will go forth on the marriage boat and let it take us down the river. You will kneel at the prow and I will be the precious rudder."

"You must give me time. I am a shy thing," said Mr. Ha-ha.

"Come, my luscious dove, let us go down that river. Let us sail loose. I have an inner weight, and we will float it away. Come, my wife, I need a spell and a spawn."

The Bride Turned into a Nanny Goat

Now we'll have a game. Now we'll have a little flimflam. Mr. Ha-ha left shyly to change into his wedding nighty and sent a nanny goat in through the door of the bedroom. The merchant turned to say *darling* and then he stopped. His wife had changed, to say the least. His wife had become a new being. Hardly the nighty. Hardly the dove. The merchant understood at once. His young wife had been transformed. His young wife, transformed by his lust, had become a nanny goat. A lecher's dish.

"I, too, am a goat," he said, "for I am a lecher and now my wife is in my own likeness."

He prodded the nanny goat with his cane. "Where is your milk, you she-beast? What could be worse than the stink of a wife? I had a mother. I had a sister. Now I have a wife. Women all, but what could be worse than this ugly muddler?" Then he saw that his marriage was a prison and rage bit him like a mosquito.

He shook the nanny goat. She vibrated in all her hairy innocence. He shook and he shook. His arms were a machine of rage. He shook her until her milk curdled. He shook her until her tongue curled up. He shook her until her lungs blew down like a balloon. He shook her until her eyes hung out like marbles. He shook and he shook. He shook his wife until she was dead.

And then he sat down on the bed at the world's end.

Fifth Entr'acte and the Nanny Goat's Funeral

There had been a death. That much was established. There had been a murder. That much was honored. The buffoons' daughters were forced to dance in order to snag him. The buffoons' daughters took lemony scarves and flashed in the blue air like terrible birds. They did the dance of the killdeer. And then suddenly they stood still. It was over. They stood so still that they looked like maypoles, their scarves still fluttering in the air like angels' breaths.

Mr. Ha-ha, the cook, stood at the side, an angel himself. He was all woman. And yet and yet he laughed a hidden laugh and rocked back and forth like a hobbyhorse. He cooed like a peace dove and the merchant saw only this cook, this luscious being. The merchant thought, Here indeed is a jam tart, a wag tail. Yes, my lovely, I choose you.

And he took him off to the wedding chamber to infect this turncoat.

In the Merchant's Bedroom

Many a story is told of the bedroom but this is an exceptional one. It may belong to legend. It may belong to fact. It begins as usual. For here we have the merchant ready and lusting.

"The wedding bells have done their ding-dong," said the merchant, "and now we are one. Come be my own. Come be my wife. One goose. One gander. I will change the world to your liking. If you but sigh, I'll bear the ground away. If you but laugh, I'll plant a garden in your mouth."

Dance of the Buffoons' Daughters

The buffoons' daughters danced a poem. What they had to say was so tiny and so fearful that they wanted you to dwell upon it. It is in the written record that they sang all at once. They sang like puppets. But they danced, believe me, like blinded children. Their dance is remembered by many countries. These are its words:

Mother died by the gun
and what of me, what of me?

Mother wore that bullet like a brooch
and then lowered herself

into her bewilderment.
When will the gun come to me?

When will I abandon myself to it
like the suicide fish to the hook?

When will the gun open like my father's ear,
open up like a cancer rose?

When will the gun open like an octopus
and close its eight legs over me?

When will the gun open like a chicken
and make me matterless and yellow?

When will the gun drown me in fur
and let me swallow the sun in a gulp?

When will the gun come like a ghost lover
and stuff me with its beanstalk?

Merchant's Arrival, Dance of Greeting
and Choosing of the Bride

Attention. This is once more a beginning. Here we have
a rich merchant. He arrived to choose a bride. The buffoons
gathered 'round for they were kin now. After all, they too had
murdered their wives. Now to the funeral. A gloomy thing,
but it could not be prevented. It was customary. And as with
all mourning, a ceremony was needed.

A funeral pyre was built. Each buffoon added his own
token. Sandalwood came, fennel and roses. A family por-

trait, a hand-carved oaken bucket, and a ship's model. None of this was jetsam. All of this was precious.

Then the merchant carried in the nanny goat, soft and supple in all her oblivion. He laid her humble body down on the funeral pyre and lit it. The fire grew quickly. It grew into a being with all its flinty language. It made the sound of the whip lashing and curling around the body. But the nanny goat could not be whipped awake. The fire did its work, eyes, mouth and belly.

No blessings were said. None were needed. It was the darker order of things.

Quarrel between Buffoon and Merchant

We have mislaid the wife. But we have not mislaid the merchant. The merchant sat in a wallow. He sat in his chair resigned to the stars' destiny. He was deep in the mystery. Deep in the labyrinth, when Mr. Ha-ha entered his chamber with seven soldiers. The soldiers were dressed in tin. They were as straight as cigarettes and as shiny as spoons. Mr. Ha-ha was dressed in all his gold paint and with a scarlet bishop's hat on his head.

"You have killed my sister," he said, "and I am her authentic mourner. You, sir, will pay. I have pitiless hands. You, sir, will pay." And the tin soldiers thumped their guns. "Where my sister walked," he went on, "roses blushed in embarrassment at her more perfect beauty. Now the roses are crippled. Now they stink like a dead goat."

"A goat she was," cried the merchant, "and I could not bear it, so I danced the killer dance. So I did her in. In this way I dried out my desire."

"And that will cost you three hundred rubles," said Mr.

Ha-ha. "You will pay until the abyss vomits her back up."

The merchant reached his hand into his money bowl and gave forth the rubles. "Now I am done paying," he said, "and the gods will not scratch their beards thinking up new griefs to deliver."

"Not at all," said Mr. Ha-ha tucking the money into his pocket. "The gods will speak to your deaf mother and tell her to turn the moon off whenever you glance up in wonder. The whippoorwills will turn to pigeons whenever you listen from your porch. And yet, good sir, I understand you, for you were altogether managed by fate. Socrates himself would have done no better."

And he turned on his heel followed by the tin soldiers.

And the merchant was left with his chilly life.

Concluding Dance

"I am a man of the people," sang Mr. Ha-ha from his throne. "A bit like the Devil himself. A bit of a rogue and a bit of a fiend. The buffoons and the merchant are guests of life. I am the host. The one who runs the clock. The one who bids hello and waves good-bye. And by the guts of Goliath I am the trickiest and the wisest man of all."

The buffoons danced ring-around-the-rosy, their hands sewed together by fate and their legs moving on a never-ending tread-mill. *Pity. Pity,* they cried out.

The merchant, his hands birds of despair, stood eating his soul. *Pity. Pity,* he cried out.

Mr. Ha-ha, the archdeceiver, said, "This is no place for pity. Every man kills his wife. It's a matter of history."

And they all danced off into the wings and ended their story.

THE LETTING DOWN OF THE HAIR

Attracting Thousands

I live in a stone room. Far from the luxury of draperies and transistors, far from the movie theaters and coffee houses, far from the men in their business suits, far from the children playing with their Lincoln Logs. I have only the daily newspapers and letters from Ruth. To tell the truth, I'm a recluse. I'm as hesitant as Emily Dickinson. Like a novice I'm all dressed in white. A recluse, yes. Yet each day I attract thousands.

The Stone Room

As I said, a stone room. Like the stones of Chile. Like the craggy rocks of Gloucester, that desperate seacoast. The steps of Rome and Michelangelo and his stone creatures. A stone room, a cupola five stories high. Like a lion in a zoo I adjust to my environment.

I came up here long ago. I didn't hide because I was ugly. I wasn't made of wolfsbane. I wasn't made of kidneys. I was made tall and of yellow hair. I'd had a normal life: men and lipstick, daiquiris and sunburns. My skin was the color of a teacup, fair but fragile. And hair, yellow-yellow hair. Brush. Brush.

A stone room as still and clean as a razor blade. All the time of the child in me this room was my secret. Oh, Mr. Man-in-the-Moon, where was your radar? Memory? Memory, here is your knife. A room to crawl into and hide. Better than the

laundry chute. Better than the broom closet. A room unused
except by birds.

Yes, as a child I would enter through a closet, standing tip-
toe on a chair, up through the trap door into the forbidden —
the dead maybe live up here, groaning every hour as they keep
watch from the lookout window. Mother can't find me, little
yellow ball. Father, you could find me if you would only look,
but Father is too sleepy to look. Else he'd come flying, come
flying. Brother, old sneak-mouth, can't find my hide-and-seek.
You'll never see. A stone room five stories up, the shape of a
merry-go-round, and eleven feet in circumference. A room like
the inside of a church bell. A chalice, a cave, a perch, queer
bird that I am. A hidden place like the inside of a seed pod.
Brush. Brush.

The Window That Watched the Pru

I have never cut my hair. That's something you ought to
know right off. It fills the room the way ten giraffes would,
twisting and twisting their long innocent necks. My hair is
innocent, too. It knows no better.

I have one window in this room and from it can see over
the countryside. The lilacs in April blushing like ten-year-old
ballet dancers. The snows of Valentine's Day laid out as
smooth and as humped as a dentist's chair. And then there
is the clock tower, striking the hour as faithful as a town crier.
But today, this May 25, the new leaves are green. They are
my green ladies. They sing. They call out to me. They are
the Christs of the grass.

But at night I watch the lights in the blackness. At night,
along with the stars, those neon jacks, I watch the Pru and
under it the skyline of Boston. The Pru stands up like an

electrified totem pole. And the planes jet over from Chicago on their way to Logan Airport. In their bellies they carry one hundred and twenty people. I am alone. I am in my room. The room is my belly. It carries me.

The Death of Everyone except Myself

Here is my mother. On my eighteenth birthday she said to me, "Why hair to the floor? Why? Every time you brush it you make me feel I'm coming out of anesthesia." But I couldn't cut it. I was faithful to my hair.

My father was indifferent. As he walked the rooms of our house he acted as if he were reading the *Wall Street Journal* on the windowpane. "It's as normal," he would say, "as coffee for breakfast. Long hair. Short hair. Who cares?"

It wasn't normal at all. It was special.

My brother, the younger, ever the teaser: "What do you want to be taken for, Lady Godiva?" My brother, the younger, ever the adorer: "Please be mine," like an old-fashioned Valentine; and then he printed it out on yellow paper: "Your hair is the color of the moon."

And Ruth. "Hey, dustmop!" as my hair caught on the legs of the antique tables. "Hey, Spanish moss," as her half-blind and adored greyhound ran after it like a string toy. Ruth the boy-child making jokes. Ruth the joker. Ruth the girl-child of two suicide attempts. Ruth the desperate and Ruth the wise, who told the world, "As the Arab said: 'Enlarge the place of thy tent.'"

Brush. Brush.

One night my hair got in the pea soup that Mother was stirring. She shouted, "The sight of you! The sight of you makes me wish I were dead!"

The next day she got her wish. She and my father out driving during a Sunday ice storm, on their way to a cocktail-brunch of caviar and bloody marys, skidded in the gray Lincoln and hit a telephone pole. They died instantly. Their necks snapped. My father's cigarette was still burning in his hand when the police arrived. They were buried side by side, heads loose, two broken dolls. Where was the blessedness? Where were the deep roots that grew me?

"You'd better cut your hair," my brother said after the funeral.

As if I could bring them back with a pair of scissors.

After that I came up to my stone room for good. But my brother didn't desert me. Little brother, now a man of sorrow, now a man in a pain hood. Yet I couldn't help him. I could only help myself. I lived in a stupor of hair. Brother pushed trays of food up through the trap door daily. I have not seen him face to face since. However, he occasionally sends notes. On the first anniversary of my parents' death the note read: *You killed them. You killed them. Moon girl, a black curse on you.*

But that was a long time ago. Yesterday a note to my middle age: *Come down, come down, you yellow-haired martyr.*

Ruth

But most of the time it's just the newspaper carefully re-folded and the mail. Envelopes addressed to the Lady of the Hair. And so forth. Letters from the people. And once in a while an aerogram from Ruth with its Japanese stamp. Ruth is my only contact with the past. Ruth my little Zen girl with her short-cropped hair. Ruth the American girl with lovers, one after the other, long after she was married. Ruth. She changed like a seascape, ever-changing, ever-embracing. No matter what it was, she was faithful to it. She was as obedient to each obsession as an old man washing his feet.

The lovers were all types. A drummer on pep pills and Ruth lapping her own pep pills' dust from the bureau drawer when she could get no more. Ruth with the foot doctor whose air conditioner gasped like a mechanical fish while they made love. Ruth with her cousin, the accountant, a precise lover, timing his thrust, she said, with a minute hand. Ruth who, after years of therapy, gave it all up for Zen. She watched her mind as a cat watches over a fish tank. She was large with her awareness; she was pregnant with her instincts. She had enlarged the place of her tent. Here in America she found the answer. "The puzzle to me is solved," she said with a new grace. And then her banker husband, First National Bank, V.P., was sent to Tokyo. Tokyo, the only city in the world with just one English-speaking psychiatrist. Or so she said. Her husband was in therapy four times a week. To be a banker was to have half a mouth. Or so she said.

Brush. Brush.

The Letting Down of the Hair

Here in my room I have my hair to care for. In the soapstone sink I wash from nine to eleven forty-five in the morning. Washerwoman, washerwoman, you make yourself dizzy. Washing this hair is a dance, a dance to be done at dawn. There is so much hair, so much sucked-up honey, that I must wash it in sections. The room becomes clammy like a sea cave, never dry. I am standing in my bare feet, dipping up and down over the sink probing the mystery. The parts that are washed sit in coils on the floor and wait patiently. It is like trying to wash sea grass. It is cumbersome and arduous and yet it is my work in life.

Then, as the clock tower chimes twelve noon, I carry it back and forth, over to the window, section by section, and hang it out the window to slap down the five stories onto the ground. I let it out to dry. I let it out to give it a life of its own. At first it hangs there like a rope, it hangs there like old yellow cereal that no one will eat. Then, if there is a hopeful wind, the breeze takes it, hair by hair, yellow by yellow. As it dries it is owned by the wind; as it dries it moves swiftly like a thousand minnows. And later when I bring it in it lies on the stone floor like wheat in a granary.

Over the years the people have gathered to watch it fall down and dry out. They call out, just as the clock strikes twelve: LADY! LADY! LET DOWN YOUR HAIR. I am becoming a tourist attraction and there is nothing I can do about it. The Gray Line bus arrives daily with a taped record-ing of facts — most of them false — about what I do and who I am. And then there is the college crowd who seem to have adopted me and one obese woman who comes each day and beats out with a stick at the children who reach for the hair and want to tug it. The people have become very devoted or very disgusted. They often write to me. I don't answer them, of course, for my hair cannot speak and it is the hair they write to. Fifty letters came just last week in response to a TV crew that came out that Monday to film the letting down of the hair. Here is a sampling of last week's letters:

Concord, N.H.

Dear Lady of the Hair,
    Your hair is haunting and moving. I love it. I couldn't see your face on our eighteen-inch screen but I could see

your hair. I could see your lovely old Victorian house.
But the psychologist on the show this morning said per-
haps that for you death was the key. He said that your
long hair is a symptom of a phobic fear of death. Don't
you know that we go on to a larger life? Don't you know
that there IS no such thing as death! There is only
change.

Dying is a glorious experience for the one it happens
to, and even for those left behind for a while it is glori-
ous if we have true understanding.

Yours sincerely,
Beatrice Engle

Acton, Mass.

Dear Crazy-Hair,
Please help to make the world saner not crazier — it's
bad enough as it is. God bless you and help you — you
need help.

Unsigned

New York, N.Y.

Dear Matchmaker —
We met at your hair up there in Mass. Joel came out
from Harvard every week of his senior year. Now we are
living together in New York. Last week he wrote a poem
to your hair but he won't send it. I wish I could write.
I'm quite illiterate and have no idea how I passed third
grade. Sometimes I think that Joel loves me. Sometimes
I think he loves you. I wish I were you. I wish I were my
doctors or my OTs or my teachers or my doctors' wives
or you. Do you know when I was, I guess, around six, I
looked at my Siamese cat and said out loud, "I wish I
was you, you're so beautiful and you don't have to wear
any clothes."

Peace.

Suzy Pearlmuter

San Francisco, Calif.

Dear Lady,

Jesus, how *do* you do it? I have been to see you
ten times, enough times for the entire universe and that
same feel of
                    Wham! Right in
the old solar plexus refuses to give up.
                              You are so beautiful
                              and I want some of that
beautifulness
          and I wanted it since a year ago when I first
found you. After last Saturday in Boston and seeing you
again I wanted it 'specially badly. And today I want it
even more.
          Lady
               can you spare
               a dime of yourself
                    for
                    Mary Jane?

Letters from Ruth

Today's mail brought a letter from Ruth, a letter and a
crucifix. It is a letter about Christ and the awful mystery. It
is a letter about the sickness unto death. "I have found Christ,"
she writes, "hours on my knees in mental prayer. All my life
I have lived in shadow. P.S.," she added, "I've even discovered
what your hair means. It is a parable for the life of a poet."

Strange. There beside the Buddha, my little Zen Ruth.
There beside that great green baby, that passive god face.
Christ. She had enlarged once more. And the crucifix was
wooden and with teeth marks on it. The greyhound puppy, of
course. I could hear her saying, My dog is Christian, too.

Ruth has Christ and I, I have only my hair. Am I like a
poet? I mean to ask her about that.

89

The Sickness unto Death

My hair is almost washed. The people are waiting down below and calling out for me. Just as I am carrying it over my brother opens the trap door and speaks. Speaks for the first time in all these years. "It's bad news," he says quietly. I stand very still, tangled in the midst of the hair. "Ruth's cousin just called. She's dead. She killed herself. First she hung the dog. And then she hung herself."

I am silent and then I say, "Thank you for telling me." And he closes down the trap door.

The sickness unto death. Enlarge the place of thy tent. Ruth dead. Ruth gone. The dog hung up like a piece of meat in a butcher shop. Ruth hung up like a thief. This change. This awful change. And I with the letter she wrote just five days ago. And the crucifix from her puppy's mouth.

The clock strikes twelve and I just stand here.

It's too late now. I wanted to ask Ruth what my life meant. Ask her about my tent. Ask her about the parable.

Now there is no one to ask. There are the people down below calling up, LADY! LADY! LET DOWN YOUR HAIR. But I could hardly ask them.

III

THE JESUS PAPERS

"And would you mock God?"
"God is not mocked except by believers."

JESUS SUCKLES

Mary, your great
white apples make me glad.
I feel your heart work its
machine and I doze like a fly.
I cough like a bird on its worm.
I'm a jelly-baby and you're my wife.
You're a rock and I the fringy algae.
You're a lily and I'm the bee that gets inside.
I close my eyes and suck you in like a fire.
I grow. I grow. I'm fattening out.
I'm a kid in a rowboat and you're the sea,
the salt, you're every fish of importance.

No. No.
All lies.
I am small
and you hold me.
You give me milk
and we are the same
and I am glad.

No. No.
All lies.
I am a truck. I run everything.
I own you.

JESUS AWAKE

It was the year
of the How To Sex Book,
the Sensuous Man and Woman were frolicking
but Jesus was fasting.
He ate His celibate life.
The ground shuddered like an ocean,
a great sexual swell under His feet.
His scrolls bit each other.
He was shrouded in gold like nausea.
Outdoors the kitties hung from their mother's tits
like sausages in a smokehouse.
Roosters cried all day, hammering for love.
Blood flowed from the kitchen pump
but He was fasting.
His sex was sewn onto Him like a medal
and His penis no longer arched with sorrow over Him.
He was fasting.
He was like a great house
with no people,
no plans.

JESUS ASLEEP

Jesus slept as still as a toy
and in His dream
He desired Mary.
His penis sang like a dog,
but He turned sharply away from that play
like a door slamming.
That door broke His heart
for He had a sore need.
He made a statue out of His need.
With His penis like a chisel
He carved the Pietà.
At this death it was important to have only one desire.
He carved this death.
He was persistent.
He died over and over again.
He swam up and up a pipe toward it,
breathing water through His gills.
He swam through stone.
He swam through the godhead
and because He had not known Mary
they were united at His death,
the cross to the woman,
in a final embrace,
poised forever
like a centerpiece.

JESUS RAISES UP THE HARLOT

The harlot squatted
with her hands over her red hair.
She was not looking for customers.
She was in a deep fear.
A delicate body clothed in red,
as red as a smashed fist
and she was bloody as well
for the townspeople were trying
to stone her to death.
Stones came at her like bees to candy
and sweet redheaded harlot that she was
she screamed out, *I never, I never.*
Rocks flew out of her mouth like pigeons
and Jesus saw this and thought to
exhume her like a mortician.

Jesus knew that a terrible sickness
dwelt in the harlot and He could lance **it**
with His two small thumbs.
He held up His hand and the stones
dropped to the ground like doughnuts.
Again He held up His hand
and the harlot came and kissed Him.
He lanced her twice. On the spot.
He lanced her twice on each breast,
pushing His thumbs in until the milk ran out,

those two boils of whoredom.
The harlot followed Jesus around like a puppy
for He had raised her up.
Now she forsook her fornications
and became His pet.
His raising her up made her feel
like a little girl again when she had a father
who brushed the dirt from her eye.
Indeed, she took hold of herself,
knowing she owed Jesus a life,
as sure-fire as a trump card.

JESUS COOKS

Jesus saw the multitudes were hungry
and He said, Oh Lord,
send down a short-order cook.
And the Lord said, Abracadabra.
Jesus took the fish,
a slim green baby,
in His right hand and said, Oh Lord,
and the Lord said,
Work on the sly
opening boxes of sardine cans.
And He did.
Fisherman, fisherman,
you make it look easy.
And lo, there were many fish.
Next Jesus held up a loaf
and said, Oh Lord,
and the Lord instructed Him
like an assembly-line baker man,
a Pied Piper of yeast,
and lo, there were many.

Jesus passed among the people
in a chef's hat
and they kissed His spoons and forks
and ate well from invisible dishes.

JESUS SUMMONS FORTH

Jesus saw Lazarus.
Lazarus was likely in heaven,
as dead as a pear
and the very same light green color.
Jesus thought to summon him
forth from his grave.
Oh hooded one, He cried,
come unto Me.
Lazarus smiled the smile of the dead
like a fool sucking on a dry stone.
Oh hooded one,
cried Jesus,
and it did no good.
The Lord spoke to Jesus
and gave Him instructions.
First Jesus put on the wrists,
then He inserted the hip bone,
He tapped in the vertebral column,
He fastened the skull down.
Lazarus was whole.
Jesus put His mouth to Lazarus's
and a current shot between them for a moment.
Then came tenderness.
Jesus rubbed all the flesh of Lazarus
and at last the heart, poor old wound,
started up in spite of itself.

Lazarus opened one eye. It was watchful.
And then Jesus picked him up
and set him upon his two sad feet.

His soul dropped down from heaven.
Thank you, said Lazarus,
for in heaven it had been no different.
In heaven there had been no change.

JESUS DIES

From up here in the crow's nest
I see a small crowd gather.
Why do you gather, my townsmen?
There is no news here.
I am not a trapeze artist.
I am busy with My dying.
Three heads lolling,
bobbing like bladders.
No news.
The soldiers down below
laughing as soldiers have done for centuries.
No news.
We are the same men,
you and I,
the same sort of nostrils,
the same sort of feet.
My bones are oiled with blood
and so are yours.
My heart pumps like a jack rabbit in a trap
and so does yours.
I want to kiss God on His nose and watch Him sneeze
and so do you.
Not out of disrespect.
Out of pique.
Out of a man-to-man thing.
I want heaven to descend and sit on My dinner plate

and so do you.
I want God to put His steaming arms around Me
and so do you.
Because we need.
Because we are sore creatures.
My townsmen,
go home now.
I will do nothing extraordinary.
I will not divide in two.
I will not pick out My white eyes.
Go now,
this is a personal matter,
a private affair and God knows
none of your business.

JESUS UNBORN

The gallowstree drops
one hundred heads upon the ground
and in Judea Jesus is unborn.

Mary is not yet with child.
Mary sits in a grove of olive trees
with the small pulse in her neck
beating. Beating the drumbeat.
The well that she dipped her pitcher into
has made her as instinctive as an animal.
Now she would like to lower herself down
like a camel and settle into the soil.
Although she is at the penultimate moment
she would like to doze fitfully like a dog.
She would like to be flattened out like the sea
when it lies down, a field of moles.
Instead a strange being leans over her
and lifts her chin firmly
and gazes at her with executioner's eyes.
Nine clocks spring open
and smash themselves against the sun.
The calendars of the world
burn if you touch them.
All this will be remembered.
Now we will have a Christ.

He covers her like a heavy door
and shuts her lifetime up
into this dump-faced day.

THE AUTHOR OF THE JESUS PAPERS
SPEAKS

In my dream
I milked a cow,
the terrible udder
like a great rubber lily
sweated in my fingers
and as I yanked,
waiting for the moon juice,
waiting for the white mother,
blood spurted from it
and covered me with shame.
Then God spoke to me and said:
People say only good things about Christmas.
If they want to say something bad,
they whisper.
So I went to the well and drew a baby
out of the hollow water.
Then God spoke to me and said:
Here. Take this gingerbread lady
and put her in your oven.
When the cow gives blood
and the Christ is born
we must all eat sacrifices.
We must all eat beautiful women.

Anne Sexton's first book, *To Bedlam and Part Way Back* (1960), and her second, *All My Pretty Ones* (1962), early established her as one of our outstanding American poets. *Live or Die* (1966) won her the Pulitzer Prize for Poetry. Her *Love Poems* appeared to wide acclaim in 1969, and her most recent book, *Transformations*, in 1971. She is the recipient of many awards and honors in poetry, here and in England.